8 95

Werner Okl

I am 7

I am anything you can think of
+ whatever I feel like at
the moment.

I AM THAT

I AM THAT

SWAMI MUKTANANDA

The Science of HAMSA
from the VIJNANA BHAIRAVA

With a preface by
SWAMI CHIDVILASANANDA

A SIDDHA YOGA PUBLICATION
PUBLISHED BY SYDA FOUNDATION

Published by SYDA Foundation
371 Brickman Rd., South Fallsburg, NY 12779-0600, USA

Acknowledgements

Grateful appreciation goes to Swami Durgananda, editor, to Beth Fountain for design, to Cheryl Crawford for cover design, to Steve Batliner and Stéphane Dehais for typesetting, and to Leonard Saphier, Osnat Shurer, Sushila Traverse, and Valerie Sensabaugh for overseeing the production of this book.

Fourth edition, second printing

Printed in the United States of America

Library of Congress Cataloging-in-Publication Data
Muktananda, Swami, 1908-
    I am that : the science of Hamsa from the Vijnana Bhairava / Swami Muktananda.
    p.   cm.
    "A Siddha Yoga publication."
    ISBN 0-914602-27-6
    1. Tantras. Rudayāmalatantra. Vijñānabhairava—Criticism, interpretation, etc.   I. Title
BL1142.6.R846M85   1992   92-35416
294.5'4—dc20   CIP

CONTENTS

SWAMI MUKTANANDA
AND THE
SIDDHA LINEAGE

Swami Muktananda

SWAMI MUKTANANDA was born in 1908, and from earliest childhood was fascinated by stories of the sages and saints. His parents lived near the South Indian city of Mangalore, and holy men often came to their home. When he was still a schoolboy, he met Bhagawan Nityananda, the ecstatic saint whom he would later recognize as his Master. Soon afterward, the boy was overcome by an intense desire for a direct experience of the Truth. And so, at the age of fifteen, he left home to begin a life of seeking. He went first to the ashram of a great Siddha Master named Siddharudha Swami. There he took initiation into *sannyāsa*, or monkhood, receiving the name Swami Muktananda, which means the "bliss of liberation." For the next thirty years he traveled the length and breadth of India, searching for the Master who could give him the experience of God. He met over sixty great beings and learned much from them. He mastered the scriptures and became proficient in hatha yoga, Ayurvedic

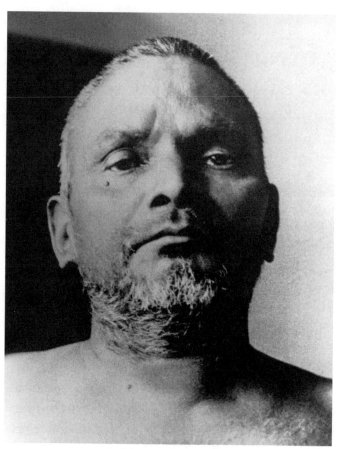

Bhagawan Nityananda

medicine, and other arts. Completely dedicated to his search, he underwent considerable difficulties and hardships, often going without food and shelter.

But the Truth he sought eluded him — until he came to the feet of the great Siddha Master whom he had met so many years before. Bhagawan Nityananda was an austere, utterly detached, overwhelmingly powerful being in whose presence all became silent. Recognizing him as the Guru he had sought, Swami Muktananda devoted himself to a life of discipleship. From Bhagawan Nityananda he received Shaktipat, the sacred initiation of the Siddha tradition, which awakened his inner Kundalini energy.

This began a nine-year period of intense internal transformation during which Swami Muktananda passed through all the stages of meditation. In 1956, he reached the culmination of his years of practice, attaining the state of Self-realization. Still, he continued to live as a simple disciple in Ganeshpuri, the small village where his Guru had settled. Then, in 1961, Bhagawan Nityananda took *mahāsamādhi* — the scriptural term for the passing of a saint. Before leaving the world, he transmitted the power of the Siddha lineage to Swami Muktananda, investing him with the full potency of his own tremendous spiritual attainment.

During the next few years, increasing numbers of spiritual seekers found their way to Swami Muktananda's ashram near Ganeshpuri. Among them were Europeans and Americans, Australians and Japanese, and soon they were inviting him to visit their countries. Baba, as he came

Swami Chidvilasananda

to be known, made his first trip abroad in 1970. This was the beginning of a remarkable worldwide mission. During three successive tours of the West, he brought what he called Siddha Yoga to hundreds of thousands of people. Empowered by his Guru to give Shaktipat initiation, Baba Muktananda awakened unprecedented numbers of people, of all ages and backgrounds, to the experience of their own inner divinity. Even people with little apparent interest in spirituality found themselves drawn by his love and attracted by the peace and power they felt in his presence.

Admired by artists and statesmen, sought out by writers and thinkers and other spiritual teachers, Baba was recognized as a figure of truly universal stature. His influence was enormous — so much so that he came to be called "the Guru's Guru." His teaching inspired people to live a life which supports the inner search, influencing thousands to look for strength and happiness within their own hearts.

During the 1970s many residential ashrams and centers for the practice of Siddha Yoga were founded, including the main SYDA Foundation ashram in the Catskill Mountains in New York State. Baba wrote and published over thirty books, established courses in yoga philosophy, and created the Siddha Meditation Intensive, the ideal environment for giving Shaktipat initiation.

For many years Baba prepared his successor, Swami Chidvilasananda. She first met him as a child of five. The loving bond of Guru and disciple was instantaneously formed, and from that time on, her development was

xvi I AM THAT

closely supervised by Baba. Later, when he made his tours of the West, Gurumayi Chidvilasananda traveled with him, serving him in innumerable ways. She translated into English his writings, as well as his lectures and the many impromptu question-and-answer sessions that he held.

In 1982, these years of rigorous preparation culminated when Baba bequeathed to her the full power and knowledge of the Siddha lineage, the vast spiritual legacy which his own Guru had passed on to him. A few months later, Baba Muktananda took mahasamadhi, merging into the ultimate state of union with the Absolute.

When Gurumayi was still a young girl, Baba said of her, "She is a great flame. One day she will illumine the world." Now, as the Master of the Siddha lineage, Gurumayi bestows the treasured gift of Shaktipat, awakening the inner energy of seekers of all nationalities. Under her guidance, the Siddha Yoga ashrams and meditation centers around the world are thriving wellsprings of spiritual life and classical yogic wisdom.

As Gurumayi travels the world, thousands of people come to meet her at public programs. Through her own joyous example she shows us how to welcome others with respect and love. Above all, in her presence the awareness of our own inner divinity can be spontaneously ignited. Once that happens, we are able to perceive that same radiant divinity everywhere.

The spiritual power and compassion of this great Siddha tradition continue to flourish in the world through the living Master, Gurumayi Chidvilasananda.

PREFACE

MOST OF US tend to take life for granted and never delve very deeply into the meaning of our existence. We look for different objects and pleasures to enrich our lives and remain unaware of the inner treasure that is ours. God dwells within us in the form of our own inner Self, but for most of us He remains concealed. In *I Am That*, Swami Muktananda explains a simple and natural means to discover that indweller. It makes use of the *prāna*, the vital force, without which we could not exist.

The *Shiva Sūtras* say: *naisargikah prānasambandhah*, "The connection of pure Consciousness with prana is natural."[1] Shaivism explains that when the divine Consciousness begins to descend into manifestation, it first transforms itself into prana, the universal life-force. The two main forms it assumes in the individual are the inhalation and exhalation. This is why the easiest way to attain union with the Divine is by taking the help of the prana, the essence of all living beings. It leads us to *pūrno'ham vimarsha*, the perfect I-consciousness, the awareness of our own Self.

In the *Bhagavad Gītā* the Lord says: *yajñānām japa-yajño'smi*, "Among sacrifices, I am the sacrifice of *japa*."[2] Japa is mental repetition of a mantra. The Lord does not say that by repeating the mantra we will attain Him, but rather that He is the syllables themselves.

The ancient scriptures of India contain a vast amount of material on japa. If a person wants to obtain certain powers or benefits, there are scriptures that indicate which mantras to repeat and the number of repetitions necessary to bring about the desired results. Most people think of japa in these terms — as a practice designed to produce concrete practical and spiritual results.

The kind of japa that Swami Muktananda taught, however, is specifically meant to put us in touch with the Self. In this book Baba, as Swami Muktananda was known to his disciples, explains at length the mantra technique of *Hamsa*, or *So'ham*.* His explanation of *Hamsa* is based on verse 24 of the *Vijñāna Bhairava*, an ancient text of Kashmir Shaiva philosophy which contains one hundred and twelve *dhāranās*, or concentration techniques, for experiencing the Self. Verse 24 is the first and most important of all these dharanas.

The mantra *So'ham* is the awareness "I am That," the

---

* *Hamsa* and *So'ham* are actually the same mantra; the syllables are reversed according to whether one inhales or exhales first. According to the grammar of the Sanskrit language, when the syllables are reversed, *so* becomes *sa*. In the Upanishadic tradition, the mantra is usually known as *So'ham*. In the Agamic, or Shaivite, tradition, it is known as *Hamsa*.

awareness of the identity between the individual soul and the Supreme. It is a mantra which we actually repeat all the time, even though we may not be aware of it. As our breath comes in, it makes the sound *ham*; and as it goes out, it makes the sound *so* or *sa*. These subtle vibrations exist within the inhalation and the exhalation just as a delicate fiber exists within a lotus stalk.

The entire cosmos is alive with sound. Fire crackles, water gurgles as it flows, and the wind sighs in the branches of the trees. Similarly, our breath naturally makes the sound *So'ham*. A person who simply watches the breath come in and go out with these syllables is doing *ajapā-japa*, the unrepeated mantra repetition.

The Indian scriptures give the name *hamsa* to the individual soul, but people now use the term colloquially. For example, when a person dies they say, "His hamsa bird left him." But they say this without understanding what hamsa truly means. *Hamsa* and *So'ham* are identical. To become aware of *So'ham*, "I am That," is to attain oneness with the supreme Self.

Whenever someone would ask Baba, "How can I know my own Self?" he would always reply, "Read my book *I Am That*."

"That's all?" the person would respond, puzzled.

"When you begin to read it," Baba would say, "you'll know why that's enough."

I remember that once Baba added, "Even after you have read it a hundred times, you will have understood only a fraction of what it contains."

There is a group of mantras known as *gāyatrī* mantras which are considered to be particularly sacred. One of these is the *Hamsa* gayatri:

hamsa hamsāya vidmahe
paramahamsāya dhīmahi
tanno hamsah prachodayāt

Let us know *Hamsa*. May that supreme *Hamsa* illumine our intellect. May *Hamsa* protect us.

The *Hamsa* gayatri is one of the traditional *sannyāsa* mantras, and in ancient times only *sannyāsis* were allowed to repeat it. In those days knowledge of the Self was reserved for the few and was considered to be beyond the reach of the ordinary person. However, Baba says that watching the breath with *Hamsa* or *So'ham* is a simple and universal technique which everyone can use. It is simply a question of becoming aware of what is already being repeated spontaneously within us. Although butter exists in milk, it manifests only after we churn the milk. Similarly, only through daily practice can we extract the power of the mantra.

Baba himself did continuous japa. Sometimes people would ask him out of curiosity, "What do you think about?"

Baba would show them his japa beads and say, "This is what I think all the time."

The *So'ham* mantra is much more than just two

syllables. It is a concentrated form of power. However, as Baba points out in this book, to truly experience its strength, we must receive it from a Guru. When we receive this mantra from a being who has become one with the source of all sound, we instantly feel its impact.

At one point during the *pattābhisheka*, the ceremony during which Swami Muktananda passed on to me the power of his lineage, he whispered *So'ham* and *aham Brahmāsmi* in my ear. I experienced the mantra as an immensely powerful force which rocketed at lightning speed throughout my bloodstream and created an upheaval in my entire system. I instantly transcended body-consciousness and became aware that all distinctions such as inner and outer were false and artificial. Everything was the same; what was within me was also without. My mind became completely blank. There was only the pulsating awareness "I am That," accompanied by great bliss and light.

When my mind again began to function, all I could think was, "What is Baba? Who is this being who looks so ordinary, yet has the capacity to transmit such an experience at will?"

I knew beyond a doubt that the mantra was God. I had never before experienced a force so mighty, yet at the same time so soothing.

Although the *So'ham* mantra is discussed in all the important scriptures of India, the technique of repeating it is explained most fully in the works of the philosophers of Kashmir Shaivism. Kashmir Shaivism, with its teaching that the world is an expansion of God and its corresponding emphasis on realizing God in the midst of ordinary life, was unquestionably the philosophy to which Baba felt closest.

For several months before he took *mahāsamādhi* and left his physical body, he spent practically all his free time absorbed in reading the *Vijñāna Bhairava*. He passed two of his last three weeks in Kashmir, on a final pilgrimage to the region which is the source of the Shaiva lineage and which has produced so many great beings.

One of the Kashmiri saints he particularly loved was Lalleshwari, who wrote many songs about *So'ham*. "As long as I failed to see my Self, I could not see the ocean even though I was drowning," she said in one of her most beautiful poems. "When I held aloft the torch of *So'ham*, I saw that I was the ocean itself."

SWAMI CHIDVILASANANDA
Gurudev Siddha Peeth
Ganeshpuri, India
December, 1982

I AM THAT

ūrdhve prāno hy adho jīvo visargātmā parochcharet
utpattidvitayasthāne bharanād bharitā sthitih

The supreme Shakti, whose nature is to create,
constantly expresses Herself upward in the form
of exhalation, and downward in the form of
inhalation. By steadily fixing the mind on either
of the two spaces between the breaths, one experiences the state of fullness of Bhairava.

VIJNANA BHAIRAVA (v. 24)

THE SELF

MAN GOES TO GREAT TROUBLE to acquire knowledge of the material world. He learns all branches of mundane science. He explores the earth, and even travels to the moon. But he never tries to find out what exists within himself. Because he is unaware of the enormous power hidden within him, he looks for support in the outer world. Because he does not know the boundless happiness that lies inside his heart, he looks for satisfaction in mundane activities and pleasures. Because he does not experience the inner love, he looks for love from others.

The truth is that the inner Self of every human being is supremely great and supremely lovable. Everything is contained in the Self. The creative power of this entire universe lies inside every one of us. The divine Principle which creates and sustains this world pulsates within us as our own Self. It scintillates in the heart and shines through all our senses. If, instead of pursuing knowledge of the outer world, we were to pursue inner knowledge, we would discover that effulgence very soon.

Without the knowledge of the Self, knowledge of outer things is like a string of zeros. Zeros are valueless until you place a numeral in front of them. In the same way, knowledge of the outer world may bring you great material benefit, but it cannot in itself bring satisfaction. As long as you are moving only on the outside, as long as you are looking for joy only in the outer world, you will never find it. But if you turn within you will experience the joy of the Self, and then you will also find that same joy outside. Real happiness, real fulfillment, comes only when you discover the Self.

To know the Self is the true aim and purpose of human life. Because a person does not understand the glory of his own Self, he gets into the habit of seeing himself as small, as imperfect, and as separate from God. In this way, he denies himself the experience of his divinity.

We pursue different spiritual practices only for the sake of experiencing this inner divinity. Yet we do not attain the Self through spiritual practices, because the Self is already attained. The Self is always with us. Just as the sun cannot be separated from its light, the Self cannot be separated from us. The power of the Self sustains our life. If the Self were not present within us, our eyes would not see, nor would our ears hear, nor would our breath come in and go out. It is because of the Self that the heart beats, that the mind thinks, discriminates, and fantasizes. It is because of the Self that love arises within us. The Self gives power to all our senses and illuminates the objects we perceive through these senses. This body does not function on its own. Without the Self, it is nothing but a corpse.

Not only does the Self pervade and sustain our own individual experience, it also pulsates in every atom of this world. In this way, the Self is apparent; it is manifest. Some philosophers say that the Self cannot be known. Yet the Self is always being experienced, at every moment of our lives.

A sage wrote: *svatantra svachchātma sphurati satatam chetasi shivah*, "The Self, Shiva, is supremely pure and independent, and you can experience it constantly sparkling within your mind."[3] It cannot be perceived by the senses, because it makes the senses function. It cannot be perceived by the mind, because it makes the mind think. Still, the Self can be known, and to know it we do not need the help of the mind or the senses.

According to Shaivism, the supreme Principle has two aspects, *prakāsha* and *vimarsha*. *Prakāsha* means "illumination," and *vimarsha* means "awareness." As prakasha that principle illuminates everything in the world, including itself. As vimarsha that principle gives knowledge about the things it illuminates and also differentiates among them. Prakasha makes us know that an object exists, and vimarsha gives us the understanding of the nature of that object. When you look at a book, it is prakasha that makes you aware that something is there and vimarsha that makes you identify it as a book and not a tape recorder. Prakasha and vimarsha exist in everything in the world. The Self is of the form of prakasha and vimarsha. It illuminates itself, and it makes itself aware of what it is.

The sun which lights the world also lights itself. In the same way, the Self which gives light to the inner and outer senses also illuminates itself. For this reason, people who have knowledge of the truth say that the Self can be known with its own light.

A poet has written, "How can the shining sun remain hidden? How can the pulsating Self, which gives radiance to all senses and to all sense objects, remain obscured?"

In the *Bhagavad Gītā* Lord Krishna says this very clearly: *buddhigrāhyam atīndriyam*, "Although it is beyond the senses, it can be known by the subtle intellect."[4] Just as we see our own reflection in a mirror, the Self can be seen reflected in the mirror of the purified intellect.

Because the Self exists equally in everything and in everyone, because it is in all objects and in all beings, because it is constantly illuminating itself, it should be very easy for us to find it in our daily lives, in the midst of our world. Truly speaking, this world is God's university, which exists to help us discover God. Whatever we do in this world is *sādhanā*. God Himself is a great *yogī*, and He created this world from His own being, from His own yoga. Therefore, it is full of yoga. All the arts, skills, and methods that are practiced in this world are nothing but yoga. Perhaps they are not completely systematic, but they are yoga. One of the main limbs of yoga is *āsana*, the sitting posture. In this world, do you always stand? Don't you sit down? Asana is a very natural part of your daily life, and that is yoga. Another of the limbs of yoga is *dhyāna*, or meditation. Meditation is nothing but concentration. Can you drive a car without concentration? Can you buy anything at the market without concentration? When you come home from the market, can you find your house without concentration? Of course, this is mundane meditation but, nonetheless, it is an aspect of yoga. All the other aspects of yoga also exist in the world. However, our understanding of the world and our attitude toward it are such that we cannot see the yoga that exists in it. Although God exists right before us, although God is manifest before us, we cannot see Him. The reason for this is that the ancient ghost of ego dwells inside us. Ego has possessed us and has made us forget our natural yoga.

What is ego? We all have the awareness of "I." It exists naturally within us, and it is pure. If we leave that "I" as it is, that "I" is God. But we always add something to the "I," and as soon as we do that, it becomes ego and causes all our troubles.

Once there was a Guru who told his disciple, "Don't become anything. Live in this world without becoming anything. If you become something, then something else will happen to torture you." One day this Guru and his disciple set out on a pilgrimage. Now, a Guru usually will not teach a disciple in a systematic way. He will not sit him down and say to him, "It is like this," or "It is like that." Instead, he will teach the disciple through a situation or through another person.

While the Guru and the disciple were on their pilgrimage, they came to the palace of a king. Outside the
palace was the king's garden, where there was a beautiful
cottage in which the king used to stay. The Guru went into
one of the rooms and lay down. The disciple asked the
Guru, "May I go to sleep in the next room?"

"Yes, you can sleep," the Guru said, "but don't
become anything."

The disciple said, "Of course I won't become
anything."

The two of them went to sleep. When they had been
sleeping for half an hour, the king arrived at the cottage
with his entourage. When he saw the mendicants sleeping
there, he became furious. "Who are you and what are
you doing here?" he cried.

This woke the disciple. "Who am I? I am a swami,"
he answered.

"What is a swami doing in the cottage of the king?"
the king shouted. He took a whip from his guard and
began to beat the disciple. He gave him thirty or forty
blows and then kicked him out of the cottage.

The king went into the next room and found the Guru
on the bed, fast asleep and snoring. "Who are you?" the
king cried.

"Hmm," said the Guru Maharaj.

"Who are you?" shouted the king again. Again, the
Guru just said, "Hmm."

"He's obviously a half-wit," the king said. "Take the
old idiot outside."

The guards carried the Guru outside and laid him down next to the disciple. The disciple was moaning and groaning. "Oh, Guruji," he said. "Look at me. Look at my predicament. I received so many blows. My back is almost broken."

"It was your own fault," the Guru said. "Why did you have to become a swami while you were sleeping on the king's bed? You received that *prasād* from the king because you became something. I did not become anything, so I did not receive the king's prasad."

This is what happens to everyone. Because you add something to your "I," to your *aham*, you receive blows from life. If you remain that pure "I," the pure I-consciousness, you are God. It is when you become a man or a woman, a swami or a professor, a doctor or an engineer that the pure "I" becomes the ego. That is how *māyā*, the delusion of ignorance, is created. Ignorance is nothing but the forgetfulness of your own Self. To forget your own Self and consider yourself something else — this is ignorance. When algae spread over the surface of water, they cover the water so that you cannot see it. When clouds form in the sky, they cover the sky so that you cannot see it. When cataracts cover the pupils of the eyes, they block your vision. In the same way, the ego acts as a screen, as a veil, which hides the Self. The shadow of ego does not allow you to know your own true nature, to see the divinity of your own Self. In the *Bhagavad Gītā*, the Lord says that although He exists in everyone as the Self, beings do not know Him. Because of ego, attachment, and delusion, people are blinded by their senses. They think that they are men or women, that they are five or six feet tall, and that this is their identity. With this understanding, they perform their actions. They forget the truth. They forget that they were born in the city of the body to do some great work. Instead, they walk on the path of the senses and are covered by their own feelings — lust, greed, anger, and so on. In this way, they become mere bound individuals, bound souls.

Truly speaking, ignorance is simply lack of understanding. If your poverty of understanding is destroyed, then you naturally expand and naturally come to know your own Self. As long as you do not know your true nature, you are a mere *jīva*, a small individual. You are a victim of death. You constantly drink the juice of jealousy, pride, and anger. But once you understand your Self, then you drink nectar — the nectar of the Self, the nectar of supreme bliss. As you turn within and your inner Shakti, your inner divine force, is awakened, you cease to be a jiva, an individual. You become Shiva, the Lord Himself.

The truth is that you already know the Self. Each person has the understanding of himself. Who will tell me that he does not know himself? Who will tell me that he is without the joy of the Self? If you have no joy, how can you live? The Self exists very naturally within you. All that you need to do is know it. It is just a matter of having the right understanding, of having the right outlook. To find the Self it is not necessary to perform difficult austerities and practices. People do so many sadhanas for

the sake of knowing the Self. Some people rigorously perform rituals and ceremonies in the name of peace, but all
they attain is effort and fatigue. Others, in the name of
yoga, hang onto techniques such as *prānāyāma*, but all
they attain is dryness. Everyone does his own sadhana
according to his own will and claims that his sadhana is
true. A yogi says, "My yoga is true." A Buddhist says, "My
Buddhism is authentic." A renunciant says, "Only my path
is right." A Sufi says, "My way is the real one."

But one thing is absolutely certain: Because the Self
exists so naturally within you, the sadhana you do to find
the Self should also be natural. It should not involve difficult austerities. It should not give trouble to your body.
It should not take you away from your home or your
family. It should not be an obstacle to your mundane
activities. Because God is not different from the world,
your sadhana should also include the world. You should
be able to practice your sadhana in this very world, easily
and with love. Although there are countless sadhanas,
countless practices, the sadhana you follow should be
a natural sadhana taught by a guide who knows that
sadhana. Not only that, it should be a sadhana in which
you experience something within. From the beginning
you should be able to catch at least a glimpse of the
Self, because only if you have recognized and experienced
God can you pursue Him and eventually attain Him.
Moreover, your path should be one which is open to
everyone. If there is any path or religion which excludes
certain people, then it cannot be a true path or a true

religion. God belongs to everyone and is within everyone. Therefore, the path you follow to attain Him should be a path which anyone can follow. It should be a path on which there are no restrictions of caste, class, age, sex, or nationality.

There is one more thing which is very important. When you begin to follow a sadhana, you should find out how many great beings have pursued that sadhana. The scriptures say that if you want to know the truth, you should follow the path the great beings pursued. Do not try to create your own path. Walk on the path that has been trod by the great beings, and then you will reach your destination.

MANTRA

THE SCRIPTURES AND THE SAINTS have described many methods for knowing the Self. Among these, the repetition of the name of God, mantra *japa*, has been called the highest path and the easiest for the present age. The mystery of mantra is very great. To know the mantra is to know God. In fact, the scriptures of Shaivism say: *mantra maheshwarah*, "Mantra is the supreme Lord." Mantra is itself the form of God: between his Name and his nature there is no difference.

The basis of mantra is sound, and sound is the origin of the cosmos. It is said: *adāu bhagavān shabda rāshih*, "God originally manifested as sound." This primordial sound is called *spanda*, or vibration. It created the universe and still pervades everywhere, continually vibrating. Even modern physicists agree that there is a vibration reverberating ceaselessly at the center of the universe. This vibration is the source not only of the universe, but of our entire being, and it pulses within us. According to Shaivism, this inner vibration is the true mantra. So the mantra is the basis of the entire world and of all beings. Therefore, it is very important to understand the subtle mystery of mantra.

Many people repeat external mantras, such as *Om Namah Shivaya* or *Hare Rama, Hare Krishna*. These mantras are all very well, but they are not the true mantra. The true mantra is not just a combination of letters and syllables. It is the inner vibration which pulses at the root of the mind. Truly speaking, only that can be called mantra which is the experience of the pure, thought-free state of the inner Self. The mantra is pure Consciousness, formless and beyond maya. It is of the form of knowledge. Within you is the pure awareness of aham, "I am." That "I am," that understanding, that pure I-consciousness, which is known as *aham vimarsha*, or the perfect I-awareness, is the pulsation of the Self and the true pulsation of the mantra. It is through this that you contemplate, perceive, and experience the supreme Principle. When the mind immerses itself in that vibration, it is the same as the mantra. The *Shiva Sutras* say that such an inner-directed mind *is* mantra: *chittam mantrah.*[5]

That inner pulsation is the source of all letters and words. All mantras spring from that pure I-awareness. When you repeat a mantra like *Om Namah Shivaya*, you are only contacting the mantra with your tongue. To know it truly, you have to get at its source, which is that inner vibration of "I am." Siddha yogis are beings who have reached this source. By repeating the mantra, they have come in contact with the Self and become established there. Therefore, the power of the Self pervades all their words.

That inner vibration, which is the source of all sound, is called by the scriptures *parāvāni* or *parāvāk*, supreme speech. The paravani level of speech exists within all of us. Ordinarily, we are aware of only one level of speech. We are aware only of the speech of our inert physical tongue, just as we are aware only of our physical body and senses. Yet the physical body is only the body of the waking state. Within the physical body is the subtle body into which we enter when we dream. Beyond that is the causal body, in which we experience deep sleep. And beyond the causal body is the supracausal body, the body of pure light, in which we experience the state of true meditation, the transcendental state called *turīya*. Just as we have these four bodies, one within the other, we also have four levels of speech, which are linked with the four bodies. The name of the gross level of speech, the speech of the physical tongue, is *vaikharī*. The second level of speech is called *madhyamā*; it corresponds to the subtle body and is located in the throat region. The third level of speech, called *pashyantī*, corresponds to the causal body and is located in the region of the heart. The fourth and highest level of speech is located in the navel region. That is paravani. Paravani is the level of sound as pure, unmanifest Consciousness, the level of the Self. It pervades everything, extending from east to west, from south to north, from above to below. It is within all of us; it is spanda, the inner creative pulsation which continually vibrates. The entire universe, with all its forms, was born from that pulsation of paravani. Infinite syllables and words and sentences exist within paravani in the form of vibration. A peacock egg contains all the colors of a peacock's feathers in a potential form. Similarly, all words and syllables exist in paravani in an undifferentiated seed form. That seed, which contains all words, is the pure aham, the perfect I-consciousness.

All mantras come out of paravani. Paravani is nothing but Parashakti, the supreme energy which creates the universe. Its nature is movement without any underlying support. The *Ishwara Pratyabhijña* says that the Self is immobile; it is always still, but paravani gives it the appearance of movement. Shiva, the supreme Reality, is completely tranquil. It is only because of his Shakti, his energy, that there is movement. It is because of Shakti that Shiva has awareness of himself. That self-awareness is aham vimarsha, the throb of pure I-consciousness, and it is from that original throb of self-awareness that the creation of the universe begins. The pure aham is paravani. So paravani is the creative pulsation of the Self. It is Kundalini, the inner spiritual energy. It is the Universal Consciousness, the all-pervading supreme Principle.

When this vibrating principle, which is very subtle at its deepest level, begins moving, it manifests through two more levels of speech, pashyanti and madhyama. The sound which exists at the level of pure vibration in paravani gradually becomes grosser. Finally, it reaches the level of vaikhari, physical speech, where it assumes the forms of different letters and syllables. So not only the mantras written in innumerable scriptures, but every letter, every sound, every word originates as the pulsation of paravani. That is why the alphabet has so much importance. It is the supreme Shakti, paravani, which has taken the form of the letters of the alphabet and which continually manifests as these sounds. The *Shiva Sūtras* say that all the letters of the alphabet are the embodiment of God. The tantric scriptures say: *mantrā varnātmakah sarve sarve varnāh shivāt-makāh*, "All mantras are composed of letters, and all letters are of the form of Shiva."[6] Each letter of the alphabet is a specific *shakti*, or power, and these shaktis taken together are known as *mātrika*. In *Shri Tantra Sadbhava* Shiva says: *sarve varnātmakā mantrās te cha shaktyātmakah priye shaktistu mātrikā jñeyā sā cha jñeyā shivātmikā*, "Mantras consist of letters, which are of the form of Shakti. Shakti manifests Herself as the alphabet. Shakti in this form should be known as matrika, and matrika should be known as being of the form of Shiva." Every letter and every word which arises from paravani is a divine mantra, because it is of the form of Shakti. That inner pulsation is one with all words. That is why words have so much power. The power of mantra repetition lies in its capacity to bring a person to a state of oneness with that inner pulsation of Consciousness. In this way, mantra has, by its very nature, the capacity to transform a person's awareness of himself as an individual into awareness of himself as Shiva.

Kashmir Shaivism speaks about two *bhāvas*, two kinds of self-identification. One is identification with the limited body and senses, and the other is identification with Shiva, the Lord himself. Living with the idea that you are just the body is called *pashubhāva*, identification as a bound soul. Identifying yourself with the Self and living with that awareness is called *shivabhāva*, identification with God. The mantra has the power to remove the limited awareness of pashubhava and make you identify yourself with Shiva. That is why it is said that all mantras are of the nature of Shiva. But the mantra you use should be one you have received from the Guru, because the mantra should be conscious. Its power should be fully awakened. It should not be inert.

As you repeat the mantra given by the Guru, its vibrations mingle with the *prāna*, the vital force. They travel to the heart, and from there they pass on to permeate all the seven constituents of the body, purifying both the body and the mind. As you repeat the mantra with pure feeling, it gradually passes from the vaikhari level to the madhyama level to the pashyanti level, and as it passes to subtler and subtler levels of speech, it purifies you on subtler and subtler levels. As you repeat the mantra with pure feeling, it takes you back to paravani. It touches the Self. It takes you to the state of the pure *aham*, the state where you and the mantra and the inner Self vibrate together as pure awareness. As long as you repeat the mantra on the gross level, you experience it as sounds and syllables. But through the Guru's grace, you pass beyond this state, and the inner divine nature of the letters is revealed.

As you repeat the mantra on the vaikhari level, the

level of gross speech, it purifies the physical body. Often during this process, you can experience the shakti of the mantra vibrating at the tip of the tongue or in the mouth. When the physical body has been purified, the mantra moves deeper inside and begins to be repeated in the throat. This means that the mantra has descended to the madhyama level, the level of the subtle body, and has begun to work there. As the mantra works at this level, you experience a divine *tandrā*, a superconscious state. This is a kind of blissful sleep, in which you may have visions of many kinds. While the mantra is going on in the subtle body, you catch glimpses of the divine nature of the mantra, and a new kind of happiness begins to arise. At this stage, the power of the mantra becomes much stronger. One repetition of the mantra at this level is equal to one hundred repetitions of the mantra at the gross level.

When the subtle body has been purified, the mantra descends to the pashyanti level. Now it goes on in the heart, which is the location of the causal body. This body is known as the seat of deep sleep. The heart is the source of the mind. It is the place where the seeds of all *samskāras*, the deep-seated impressions which cause us to go round and round on the wheel of bondage, are stored. As the mantra goes on at this level, the subtle seeds of these impressions are purified. When the mantra is being repeated at the level of the causal body, you get into a state of intense intoxication, and wave after wave of ecstasy is released.

At last, when the causal body has been completely

purified, the mantra descends to the navel region, to the level of paravani. It touches the Self. It takes you to the state of the pure aham, the state where you and the mantra and the inner Self vibrate together as pure awareness. Now the light of the Self begins to reveal itself. At this level, the mantra is no longer repeated deliberately. Instead, it is experienced going on within as the pure throb of the perfect I-awareness, the divine pulsation of the supreme Shakti. In fact, japa (mantra repetition) at the level of paravani is simply the throbbing awareness of *purno'ham*, the awareness "I am perfect." It is the experience of the pure Consciousness, the pure Self.

A great being said:

Receive the mantra from a Guru, and then realize
    the eternal Absolute.
That mantra will wash away all your sins
    and impurities.
It will reveal to you the all-pervasive God,
    who blazes within in the form of brilliant light.
Repeat that mantra day in and day out.
Do not forget it even in your dreams.
Not a single breath should go out or come in
    without the repetition of the mantra.
Then no matter where you go you will hear
    that mantra.
You will hear it emanating from the sky, from the air,
    from everything.
You will realize that all sentient beings and even

inert objects repeat the mantra.
You will hear the pulsation of that sound everywhere.
Without fear and hatred, repeat the mantra.
As you repeat the mantra you will see the Lord of the
universe everywhere.

The mantra has great power. The mantra is God. The world and everything in it are the embodiment of the mantra. Even your prana goes in and out through the power of the mantra. Life is the mantra. Therefore, get in touch with the mantra. It always pulsates within. All you have to do is hear it.

HAMSA

THE MANTRA TECHNIQUE I am going to describe is the teaching of the Siddhas, the highest of all spiritual techniques. It gives the direct experience of the Self. Its knowledge has been passed down from Guru to disciple in unbroken lineage. If a person receives this mantra from a Siddha Guru and practices it according to the Guru's instructions, he also attains the state of perfection, the state of a Siddha.

The specialty of *Hamsa* is that it works for anyone. It can be practiced very easily and naturally by young people or old people, by people of every country and every religion. You can practice it while living an ordinary life in the world. Through the science of the *Hamsa* mantra, you attain that by which everything is attained, you perceive that by which everything is perceived, you know that by which everything is known.

Hamsa is the natural mantra. There are many mantras that you repeat with your tongue, many mantras that you repeat on the beads of a japa *mala*. But *Hamsa* is not like these. *Hamsa* mantra emanates spontaneously from within you; it repeats itself naturally along with your breathing. For this reason, it is called your own mantra or the mantra of the Self. The Vedas have given a high place to this mantra. The Tantra *shastras,* too, have given it an important position. The great beings, the Siddhas, sing of it in their poetry.

The science of *Hamsa* is revealed in the *Vijñāna Bhairava,* one of the supreme scriptures of Shaivism. In India there is a tradition that no matter what you say in the spiritual field, you must have an authority to prove the truth of it. That authority is the scriptures. If you make any sort of statement about spirituality, people will ask you, "What is the philosophical foundation of your words?" If you say that your statement is not founded on any philosophy, then people will tell you that they do not accept what you say. Even though your words may be true, even though they may be genuine, if you cannot give the proof of any scripture or philosophy, then what you say cannot be accepted.

The *Vijñāna Bhairava* is one of the highest scriptures. It is quoted by other scriptural authors when they want to give a final testimony to the truth of what they say. Every scripture must have been composed by someone; it must have an expounder. The *Vijñāna Bhairava* is no exception. *Vijñāna Bhairava* means "the wisdom of Bhairava." It is an *agama,* a scripture that comes from the mouth of the supreme Principle of the universe, Shiva, who is also known as Shankara or Bhairava. Even though it is a scripture of India, it does not belong to India or to any other particular country or caste. It belongs only to Consciousness, and it deals only with Consciousness. It describes how the supreme Principle, your own inner Self, can be attained.

The *Vijñāna Bhairava* is in the form of a dialogue between a Guru and a disciple. The Guru is Bhairava. The disciple is his consort, Bhairavi, the mother of the world, who is also called Shakti, Shiva's creative energy. So this is a dialogue between a husband and a wife, between the supreme Lord and his beloved.

After hearing Bhairava describe the state of the formless supreme Reality, Bhairavi asks him to reveal to her a simple means of knowing that supreme and secret inner Principle. Her question is of great benefit to all people. In this age, when it is very difficult for people to pursue rigorous practices and austerities, it is absolutely necessary that we find a path which we can follow easily and naturally, without giving up our worldly lives, without abandoning our jobs or families, without having to put forth too strenuous an effort. For this reason, Bhairavi's question is very helpful to everyone. The Lord replies to it by explaining 112 easy techniques for attaining the truth. These techniques are called *dhāranās*. A dharana is an awareness through which you hold God within. The *Vijñāna Bhairava* is made up of dharanas. Of these, the first is the most sublime. It is very beautiful, and it is very natural. It is the awareness of *Hamsa*, which everyone has within himself.

This small book that I have written is a commentary on that dharana. Read it with great subtlety, going deeper and deeper inside. If you truly understand these words, then you will come to know your own divinity.

* * *

Shiva says: *ūrdhve prāno hy adho jīvo visargātmā parochcharet/utpattidvitayasthāne bharanād bharitā sthitih,* "The supreme Goddess, whose nature is to create, ceaselessly expresses Herself upward from the center of the body in the form of exhalation and downward in the form of inhalation."[7]

Sit quietly, and watch the going out and coming in of the breath. The outgoing breath is called *prāna,* and the ingoing breath is called *apāna.* Apana is also called *jīva,* the individual soul, because only when the apana enters the body can it be said that the soul is in the body. If the prana goes out and the apana does not come back in, then the body is nothing but a corpse. When the apana comes in, it moves downward toward the heart. When the prana goes out, it moves upward. In this way, the breath keeps arising and subsiding. As the breath comes in and goes out, it makes a sound. When it comes in, it makes the sound *ham,* and when it goes out, it makes the sound *sa.* The sound of the breath coming in and going out is the repetition of *Hamsa* mantra.

This is what you must understand about *Hamsa* mantra.

It is natural japa, natural mantra repetition. Whether we are aware of it or not, this mantra is always going on. It goes on not only in us, but in all living creatures, and it is because of its pulsation that all creatures are alive. In a human being, the breath comes in and goes out 21,600 times a day, and each time it repeats this mantra. We may think we are repeating the mantra at certain times, but in reality it goes on spontaneously, 21,600 times a day. This is how enlightened beings understand mantra repetition. The great saint Kabir described this natural japa in one of his poems, saying, "I am not repeating the mantra on my beads, nor am I repeating it with my tongue. God Himself is repeating my mantra, while I sit in a very relaxed manner and listen to it."

This is known as *ajapā-japa*, unrepeated mantra repetition. Ordinary people practice external japa, in which they repeat the mantra out loud or in the mind. But inside us, this natural mantra is taking place. One who simply watches the breath, being aware that it is coming in and going out with the sounds *ham* and *sa*, is pursuing ajapa-japa. This is the true way of practicing *Hamsa* mantra.

Hamsa is also known as *ajapā gāyatrī*, the unrepeated gayatri mantra. It is the self-born mantra. No sage invented it. It was not composed by any yogi. The Lord Himself initiates us into this mantra when we are in our mother's womb. It is said in the *Garbha Upanishad* that when the fetus in the womb is seven months old, the soul receives knowledge of its past and future. It knows who it has been and who it will be. When the movie of its lives passes before its mind, it becomes frightened and begins moving restlessly here and there. But in whichever direction the fetus tries to move, it runs into trouble. When it moves upward, it comes up against the stomach. There, it is burned by the gastric fire. It moves away and bumps into the kidney. The kidney is very salty, and when the fetus receives the shock of that, it moves away again. But when it moves away from the kidney, it comes up against the intestines, which stink. In this way, it keeps moving all the time, and wherever it moves, a new difficulty arises to welcome it. Finally, the fetus becomes desperate and begins to call out to God for help.

Now God, the Self, is right there. He has been watching all of this, and when at last the soul starts crying out and taking refuge in Him, God bestows His grace upon it. He gives it instruction in *So'ham*, which means "That am I" and which is the same as *Hamsa* mantra.*

As the fetus repeats the mantra, it begins to understand its identity with the supreme Principle. It becomes immersed in the *So'ham* awareness, the awareness of its true nature, and becomes calm and serene. However, when nine months are over, the fetus is forcibly ejected from the mother's womb. The moment it comes out, it begins crying, making the sound "Kwanh, kwanh," or *ko'ham, ko'ham*. It forgets God's instructions and the understanding it has attained. It forgets the awareness of *So'ham*, and cries, "*Ko'ham* — who am I?" From that moment, it begins

---

* See note, page xx.

to identify itself in different ways, saying, "I am this body," "I belong to a particular class," "I am a woman," "I am a man," "I am a sinner." It becomes established in this kind of understanding and lives its life accordingly.

Yet all the time, *Hamsa* is going on. When the child comes out of the womb, it first breathes out and then breathes in with the sound *ham*. From then on, the mantra keeps repeating itself. Because a person does not remember that he has been initiated into the mantra, he has to go to a Guru and receive initiation again. However, the mantra is already going on inside; all he really has to do is become aware of it.

To understand the secret of *Hamsa*, you first have to understand the secret of prana. You should never underestimate the value of prana. Prana is the vital force.* It is a divine object of your life. Prana is the support of your body; once the prana leaves the body, the body becomes a mere corpse, which no one wants to look at. In fact, not only is prana the support of human life, it is the vital force of the entire universe. It pervades and supports the entire world. All beings are alive because of prana. Even trees and mountains exist with its support. Shaivism says, "From Shiva to an ant, everything lives because of prana."

Although prana is one, within the human body it takes five forms, known as prana, apana, *samāna, vyāna,* and *udāna*. In these five forms it flows through the system

---

* The word *prāna* has two different meanings. It is a general term referring to the vital force of the universe and also a technical term referring to the exhalation.

of 720,000 *nādīs*, or bodily channels, and carries on all the life processes. Everything depends on prana. A scriptural author says: *sarvam prāne pratishthitam*, "Prana is life itself." When the prana stops moving in and out of the body, there is either *samādhi* or death.

With whose support does the prana move in and out? It is not we who bring the breath in and out of the body. The breathing process takes place on its own, by the will of God. What would happen to us if the breath were to come inside and stop in the heart? This does not happen, because there is a force which will not allow the breath to stop inside. Even if we want it to stop, that force pushes it out. In the same way, when the breath arises and goes out of the body, it does not stay outside. There is something which sucks it inside. The force that makes the breath go in and out is the supreme Consciousness, the supreme energy. The same Consciousness which creates the universe also pushes the breath in and out. In fact, the scriptures tell us that it is that very universal Consciousness itself that comes in and goes out as the breath. The Upanishads say that prana is God. Shaivism says: *prak samvit prāne parinatā*, "Universal Consciousness becomes prana."[8] In the process of creating the world, the supreme Consciousness evolves into prana and enters everything. On the one hand it becomes sound. On the other hand it becomes prana. It is the same supreme Consciousness which has become our own prana, our own vital force. So the sound the breath makes as it flows in and out of the body is the utterance of the supreme Consciousness, the universal energy, which creates the universe out of its own being and which, when it resides in the human body, is known as Kundalini. This is what Shiva says in the *Vijñāna Bhairava*. Kundalini itself is repeating the mantra *Hamsa*. *Hamsa* is the actual sound of God.

This utterance of the supreme Consciousness, which goes on continually and which we know as inhalation and exhalation, vibrates. I have already explained that according to Shaivism, it is this vibration which creates the inner and outer worlds. The universe has manifested out of *shabdabrahman*, the original vibration, the primordial divine sound. The primordial sound *Om* gives rise to the two syllables *sa* and *ham*, and from these two syllables the universe is born. So the two syllables which the inner Consciousness utters as it brings the breath in and out of the body are the original sound vibration that manifests the cosmos.

According to Shaivism, the manifest world is made up of different vibrations, different combinations of sounds. The sounds which form the basis of the world are the sounds of the fifty-two letters of the Sanskrit alphabet. In the process of creating the world, the power of Consciousness manifests as these different sound syllables, which we know as the different letters of the alphabet. These letters are called *mātrikās*. When it takes the form of the letters, the supreme Consciousness is called *mātrikā shakti*, the power of letters. That group of letters, the matrika, is the cause of all knowledge and all understanding and the cause of the creation of the inner and outer worlds. *Ham* and *sa* are the source of all these letters; all the other sound syllables arise from the two syllables *ham* and *sa*. So *ham* and *sa*, which arise and subside with the prana, are actually the source of the universe. The entire world is of the form of the words which have emanated from these two syllables. The *Guru Gītā* says, "*Ham* and *sa* are the source of the world."

In the *Shiva Sūtras*, there is an aphorism: *jñānā-dhishthānam mātrikā*, "Matrika, the power of sound inherent in the alphabet, is the source of limited knowledge."[9] Limited knowledge is dualistic knowledge, worldly knowledge, the knowledge of differences. Matrika is the source of all this knowledge. It is the source of all language, all scriptures, all poetry. Through the workings of the matrika shakti, letters form words, words form sentences, sentences have meaning and give rise to understanding. Words give rise to all our feelings. Whatever we think and feel, we think and feel through the power of words. Through words we experience the dualities of pleasure and pain, good and evil, virtue and sin. If someone calls you a sinner, you feel insulted and ashamed. But if someone calls you a good person, you become happy. This is the duality created by words, and because of this duality you suffer or experience happiness. Yet all these feelings and states are nothing more than the play of the two syllables *ham* and *sa*, because all words have emanated from them.

It is because you do not understand the true nature of the letters that you are bound by them. When you understand their true nature, they no longer have the power to bind you. To understand these two syllables, *ham* and *sa*, as they really are is liberation. *Ham*, the sound which comes in with the inhalation, is Shiva, the pure I-consciousness, the inner Self. *Sa*, which goes out with the exhalation, is Shakti, God's creative energy. The *Spanda Kārikās* say that the first throb, the first movement of Shakti, is called *sa*. Inhalation and exhalation are the dance of Shiva and Shakti, of God and His creative energy. As the supreme energy comes in, it makes the sound *ham*. As it goes out, it makes the sound *sa*. In this way, it creates and dissolves infinite worlds. If you perceive this with true understanding, you realize the Truth immediately. By understanding the mystery of *Hamsa*, you come to know the Self.

The poet Sundardas said, "The Self is God, the Self is Consciousness, and the Self is always repeating its own mantra, *So'ham, So'ham.*" The mantra *Hamsa* is the source of all knowledge. Therefore, to obtain knowledge, you should repeat it. The poet Kalidas, who knew the mystery of words, said that whether in mundane or spiritual life, we cannot understand anything without using words. Without words, we cannot carry on any of our activities. Even mute people use sign language to communicate with one another. We can describe an object only when it has a name, only when letters are combined into words and have a meaning. In mundane life, the word conveys knowledge of an object and therefore is one with that object. In the same way, knowledge of God is contained in these two syllables, *ham* and *sa*.

However, if you want this mantra to bear fruit for you, you must understand it in the right way. Everyone in the world repeats *Hamsa*, but most people do not gain its fruit. This is because no one has the right understanding about it. Shaivism says: *prithak mantrah prithak mantrī na siddhyanti kadāchana*, "If the mantra is kept separate from the repeater of the mantra and its goal, one cannot attain the fruit of the mantra."[10] There should not be any feeling of duality between the mantra and the repeater of the mantra. In the practice of *Hamsa*, the mantra takes place on its own, and the goal of the mantra is the Self. It is That which repeats it, it is That which is its goal, and it is That which is attained by repeating it. When the mantra, the repeater of the mantra, and the goal of the mantra become one and the same for you, you attain the fruit of the mantra. This is the method of practicing the mantra. Eknath Maharaj used to say, "I am God, I am the devotee, and I am the articles of worship." In the same way, when you practice *Hamsa* mantra, you should remember that you are the mantra and the goal of the mantra. You should always remember that you are *Paramahamsa*, you are Shiva, you are the Lord Himself.

Shaivism says that the contemplation of *So'ham* is the contemplation of your own true nature. It is the knowledge of your own Self. Therefore, you should realize this japa in all your activities. Until you understand that the mantra is going on within you, you can repeat it. As you repeat it, sitting quietly and combining the two syllables with the breath, you will eventually begin to understand that it is happening on its own. You will begin to hear it coming in and going out with the breath.

But it is not enough just to hear the mantra. There is more to the *Hamsa* awareness. You should understand this very clearly, because it is a mystery which only one with a sharp and subtle intelligence can grasp. As you watch the breath coming in and going out, you will become aware that when it comes in, it comes in to a distance of twelve fingers and merges. The place where it merges is called *hridaya*, the heart, or the inner *dvādashānta*. It is also called the Shiva dvadashanta. The breath merges here, and then it arises again and goes out to a distance of twelve fingers and merges in the space outside. That outer space is called the outer dvadashanta, the Shakti dvadashanta, or the external heart. Here, "heart" does not refer to the physical organ. The heart is the place where the breath merges, inside and outside. In reality, these two places are one. The duality of inner and outer space exists only because you have the sense of your physical body. The moment you transcend your body-consciousness, the inner and outer spaces merge. This happens naturally as you pursue *Hamsa*.

When the breath comes in with the sound *ham* and merges inside, there is a fraction of a moment which is completely still and free of thought. This is the *madhya-dashā*, the space between the breaths. This is where you have to focus in meditation. To focus on that space is the highest meditation and the highest knowledge. That still space between the breaths, that space where no thoughts exist, is the true goal of the mantra. It is a miraculous space. It is *aham vimarsha*, the inner pulsation of Consciousness. It is from this space that all words arise and subside. It is this space without form which pulls the apana inside and which pushes the prana out. This space where *ham* merges inside, before *sa* has arisen, is the space of God, of supreme Consciousness, of the Self. The place where *sa* merges outside is equally the place of God. So realize that moment of the merging of the two syllables. If you come to know that moment, if you become established in it, you experience the Truth.

This is *hamsa vidyā*, the science of *Hamsa*. Not only is it natural mantra repetition, it is natural pranayama. The yoga scriptures mention many different forms of pranayama, regulation of breath, and *kumbhaka*, suspension of breath. Yogis practice pranayama in order to quiet the mind. They practice kumbhaka because when the breathing is suspended, one gets into samadhi. But Shaivism says that pranayama and kumbhaka should happen naturally, through the inspiration of God. In fact, they are happening automatically. Who does not do pranayama? Day and night, continuously, inhalation, exhalation, and suspension of breath are taking place. This is natural pranayama, natural kumbhaka. So there is no need for you to practice any special technique of pranayama. You should just try to understand what is happening with the breath. You should not try to do anything. There is no need for you to regulate your breathing. Just let it come in and go out naturally. There is no need for you to try to

suspend your breath. You just have to become aware of
the space that already exists between the breaths. The
state of stillness that occurs when the syllables merge
inside and outside is natural kumbhaka. As you practice
Hamsa, the time of the suspension of breath automatically
begins to extend itself. The duration of the kumbhaka
increases naturally. As long as the breath is suspended, you
experience the Self. This is the state of samadhi. From that
arises perfect bliss.

The purpose of practicing *Hamsa* mantra is to attain
that state where the breath merges. That is called the
natural state, the state in which kumbhaka takes place on
its own. This is natural yoga. It is the yoga of the Siddhas,
and it is supreme. It is meant for a very intelligent person,
for even though it is very natural, only a person with great
understanding can attain it.

There was a great saint named Ranganath Maharaj
who said, "Not everyone can learn the skill of merging in
That. It is very easy, yet not everyone knows how to
become absorbed in the Self naturally and spontaneously."
He went on to say, "Only one who has the grace of the
Guru can attain this skill, which cuts asunder the noose of
worldliness."

It is not that you have to attain that kumbhaka for an
hour or two. Even to attain it for a second is more than
enough. The scriptural authors have measured the value
of that still moment when the breath merges. They have
said that to sing God's glory one million times is equal to
saying the mantra once, but that to repeat the mantra one

million times is equal to one second of the meditation in which you merge in the space of stillness. That space is supremely silent. In that space there are no thoughts, no imaginings, no feelings. It is completely free of forms and attributes. In that state there is no pain, no pleasure, no dullness, no ignorance. That is the state of the supreme Truth. It is turiya, the transcendental state. It is the highest state, the highest yoga. That moment when merging takes place, that moment of natural kumbhaka, that moment when *ham* goes away and *sa* has not yet arisen, is the true mantra — not even the two syllables *ham* and *sa*, but that merging space, is the true mantra.

Sometimes people are confused about whether to repeat the mantra as *Hamsa* or *So'ham*, but there is no reason for confusion, because *Hamsa* is *So'ham* and *So'ham* is *Hamsa*. There is no difference in the syllables or in the meaning; it is only that the syllables are reversed. *Hamsa* means "I am That." *So'ham* means "That am I." There is no difference. So you can use whichever form of the mantra you like, whichever form the Guru gives, repeating *ham* on the inbreath and *so* or *sa* on the outbreath. What is important is that you come to know the space where the two syllables arise and subside. That is the state of God, and you take the help of the two syllables just to attain that state. Until you get into that state where the syllables merge, keep repeating the mantra. But know that the true goal of the mantra is that awareness.

Once King Janaka was sitting on the bank of a river, repeating *So'ham* at the top of his voice. A sage named

Ashtavakra happened to be passing by. He was a great knower of Truth, an enlightened being. When he saw Janaka, he was surprised. He knew that Janaka was a great being. He was known as Videhi Janaka, the one who has gone beyond body-consciousness. Although he ruled his kingdom, he did so from the state beyond identification with the body. So Ashtavakra wondered why Janaka was repeating So'ham, So'ham in this manner.

As I said before, great beings do not teach only through philosophical discourses. They teach in whatever way they feel like teaching, and they may use any means to make their point. Ashtavakra watched Janaka for a while, wondering how he should instruct him. Then he had an idea. He sat down. In one hand he had a water bowl, and in the other hand he had a yoga-danda, the T-shaped stick that yogis use for support in meditation. He began to say very loudly, "This is my water bowl; this is my yoga stick! This is my water bowl; this is my yoga stick!"

King Janaka began repeating his mantra louder. The sage also began to repeat his mantra louder. After a while, King Janaka became annoyed. He opened his eyes and asked, "O brother, what are you doing?"

"What are you doing?" asked Ashtavakra.

"I am repeating the mantra So'ham," Janaka said.

Ashtavakra said, "I am also repeating a mantra. I am repeating, 'This is my water bowl; this is my yoga stick.'"

The king said, "Have you lost your brains? Who told you that the water bowl and the stick don't belong to you?

Why do you have to keep shouting about it?"

The sage replied, "It seems to me that you are the one who lacks understanding. Who told you that you are not That? Why do you have to go on shouting that you are That?"

When Janaka heard this, he suddenly understood the truth. He realized that he was That. He understood that he did not need to go on repeating *So'ham*, that he only needed to understand it.

This is what you also need to understand. *Hamsa* is not a mantra that you merely repeat. What you have to do is become established in the awareness of the mantra going on inside you, in the goal of the mantra, in the pulsation which exists in the space where the syllables arise and subside. When I say, "Meditate on your own Self," this is what I mean. To meditate on your Self means to attain this space.

People often talk about meditation, and to learn meditation they pursue so many different techniques. They undergo so many difficulties trying to learn how to meditate, and when they do not succeed, so many doubts come into their minds. Therefore, first of all, you must understand the meaning of meditation. Real meditation is a state completely free of thoughts. This is how the great sage Maharishi Patanjali defined meditation in his *Yoga Sūtras: yogashchitta vritti nirodhah*, "Yoga is to still the movements of the mind."[11] Meditation does not mean holding a certain object in the mind. If you think this is what meditation is, then you are insulting meditation. Meditation should happen very naturally. It should be completely spontaneous. This space that you attain when the prana goes out and dissolves and when the apana comes in and dissolves, this space where there is no thought, no object, is true meditation. It is natural meditation, the highest meditation.

Jnaneshwar Maharaj said, "The true meaning of meditation is to do nothing." This does not mean that you should become lazy and just lie down in any way you like. To do nothing means to be without any object in meditation. Many people complain to me that they do not have visions during meditation, that nothing happens to them. They say, "I don't see any flames, any colors, or any lights." Yet it is that "nothing" which is the real state of meditation. Truly speaking, if you see anything in your meditation, then your meditation is worldly; it is of the world. Only that complete stillness where there is no thought in the mind is real meditation.

So *Hamsa* is natural meditation. It is the highest knowledge. It is not a religion. It is not a sect. It is neither Hinduism nor Christianity nor Islam. It is the "ism" of the pure I-consciousness, the "ism" of your own Self. It is very spontaneous and completely true. All the Siddhas have said that there is no greater knowledge than the knowledge of *Hamsa*, no greater japa than ajapa-japa, no greater worship than the uniting of *ham* and *sa*.

In Delhi, there was a great being named Sundardas. He said, "Day in and day out, the breath comes in and goes out with *So'ham, So'ham.* Use the mala of the prana and repeat it all the time. What can you attain by using wooden beads? If you repeat this ceaselessly, it cools down all your different kinds of anguish." Sundardas went on to say, "With this mantra, the Self is constantly worshiping itself." People have their own interests, and according to their interests they worship different deities. But true worship is the understanding of the inner *ham* and the outer *sa*. This mantra is the same for everybody. No matter which country you come from, no matter which religion you follow, this natural awareness of "I am That" exists for you. Different philosophies may use different words for the mantra; people may hear the sounds of the syllables in different ways. In Sufism, they hear them as *Ya Hu*. In Tibetan Buddhism, they hear them as *Hung So*. But all these are really the same mantra. This mantra is beyond the body, beyond the senses, beyond the four psychic instruments. It comes from paravani, the deepest level of speech; it emanates spontaneously with the breath.

A true yogi is one who does this natural pranayama, uniting his incoming and outgoing breaths with the syllables *ham* and *sa* and performing this natural japa, ajapa-japa. In this way, a yogi brings himself and God together; he unites himself with the Self from which he has become separated. There are people who do a few postures and pranayama and call themselves yogis, but they are not true yogis. A true yogi is one who becomes established in his own Self with the awareness of *Hamsa*, of "I am That." Jnaneshwar Maharaj said, "The king of yogis takes repose in the space between *ham* and *sa*." Once a person is

established there, meditation goes on continually, whatever he is doing.

Kabir wrote: *so'ham ajapa jāp, chhute punya aur pāp*,
"The unrepeated mantra repetition, *So'ham*, destroys all
your sins and virtues." The *So'ham* awareness is also
described as the awareness *aham Brahmāsmi*, "I am the Absolute," or *tat tvam asi*, "Thou art That." It is the understanding of your identity with the supreme Principle, and
this understanding has the power to destroy all of your
accumulated karmas and past impressions. Not only does
it destroy the effects of millions of sins, it also cuts the
bondage which arises from your good actions. Most
people want to eliminate the effects of their bad actions,
not realizing that their virtues are just as binding as their
sins. Your sins bind you with an iron chain and your virtues
with a golden one. That is the only difference between
them. If you want liberation, both sin and virtue must be
wiped out, and that is what happens when you attain the
awareness of *So'ham*. This awareness puts an end to the
cycle of birth and death, killing the notion of duality.

As long as you have the feeling of duality, the feeling
that one human being is different from another, that one
class is different from another, you cannot experience real
happiness. The sense of otherness is the source of all fear,
of all suffering, and of all sin. However, as you practice
Hamsa, the consciousness of equality dawns in a natural
manner.

The mind and the breathing are intimately con-
nected, for it is the movement of prana which creates the

countless universes that arise and subside in the mind.
When the breath is uneven, the mind becomes disturbed,
and the sense of duality arises. As the breath becomes
even, the mind automatically becomes still. Ordinary people often breathe rapidly, and their outgoing breath is
expelled for a long distance. This indicates an outgoing
mind. As the mantra goes deeper, the breathing slows, and
the outgoing breath becomes shorter. The incoming and
outgoing breaths become even, and as this happens, the
mind and senses turn inward, toward the Self.

The purpose of all the pranayama that hatha yogis
perform is to balance the duration of inhalation and exhalation, because this balance quiets the mind and brings
the awareness of equality. This happens very easily and
naturally through the practice of *Hamsa*.

As you become aware of *Hamsa*, the breath naturally
begins to come in and go out to the same distance and for
the same length of time. The spontaneous suspension of
breath which I have already described happens automatically. In the still space where the breath merges, the feeling
of duality disappears, and you become conscious of the
equality of all things. Jnaneshwar Maharaj said: *tain shar-
irabhavāva nāshati indriyen vishaya visarati jain so'ham bhāva
pratiti prakata hoye,* "As you become aware of So'ham, the
body-consciousness dissolves, and the senses, which have
been wandering among outer objects, automatically turn
within." Then you experience the union of Shiva and
Shakti within yourself. Outside and inside become one.

The syllable *ham*, which comes in with the apana, is

the seed mantra of the Self. Whether we know it or not, we are always aware of this syllable. We always say, "I, I, I." Truly speaking, our real identity is *Hamsa*. That is our real humanity. The embodied Self, which experiences itself as "I," is really the divine Self. But although we are all aware of the first syllable, even though we always say, "I," we have given up the awareness of the second syllable. We have given up the understanding of That. And because we give up the awareness of That, which is the awareness of the Self, we forget our real identity and begin attaching our "I" to different things. We begin to say, "I am a man," "I am a woman," "I am an officer," "I am a Republican," "I am a rich person." Then we begin to say, "My husband, my wife, my cat, my dog, my body." Our "I" becomes the "I" of the petty ego, which identifies itself with the body and senses.

Yet as soon as we understand the second syllable, as soon as we understand that we are That, then our "I" becomes free of association and totally pure. It becomes the true aham, aham vimarsha, the pure I-consciousness. The ordinary "I" is Consciousness in bondage. The pure "I" is Consciousness in the state of liberation.

As you repeat *Hamsa* with the understanding of the perfect aham, this realization dawns. When you begin to have the awareness of this pure "I," the intellect, too, becomes purified, and then you are able to perceive God shining within. The knowledge that you are the Self arises spontaneously within you. The moment you perceive the supreme Principle in the mantra, you are liberated. The mantra of pure I-consciousness destroys the duality of this world and reveals that God who is one. Jnaneshwar Maharaj said: *paim pratibimbauni bimbaverīm prabhechī jaisī ujirī te so'ham vritti avādharīm, taisī hoye aiseni maga parasparem, te so'ham drishti jaim avatare taim tiye hī sakata sare, āpaiseyā,* "Just as light pervades everywhere, the *So'ham* consciousness extends from the embodied Self to the supreme Self. When man becomes fully immersed in the *So'ham* vision, he spontaneously merges in the supreme Being."

Knowledge of God is a matter of understanding. You do not have to make an effort to find God, because there is no place where God is not. He is not something you are going to attain; you have simply to become aware of Him. Jnaneshwar asked, "To know that a person is your father, how long do you have to repeat the mantra 'He is my father, he is my father'? Your mother just says, 'Child, look, here is your father,' and immediately you understand it. How much effort do you have to make?" The scriptures and the saints are like a mother. When they say, "You are That," how long should it take you to know That?

In the same way, the science of *Hamsa* is a matter of awareness. It is the highest sadhana because you do not do the practice; you simply become aware that the practice is happening on its own. Although it is very simple, the yoga of *Hamsa* encompasses all other yogas; all other yogas depend on it.

The *Guru Gītā* says: *ham bījam,* "Ham is the seed." In the seed of the Self the entire universe is contained. In the same way, *Hamsa* mantra is the seed of all spiritual practices. Just as a huge banyan tree springs from a tiny seed and contains branches, roots, leaves, flowers, fruit, and thousands of other seeds, the seed of *Hamsa* contains yoga, meditation, japa, austerities, and all powers.

There are many philosophies, many teachings, and many traditions, but of all these, the two syllables *ham* and *sa* are the only things you really need to keep with you. The great saint Sundardas said, "Give up everything else; keep only these two syllables."

You can practice *Hamsa* whether you are walking or sitting, eating or sleeping. You can practice it no matter what you are doing. The great being Brahmananda said:

> O *sādhus*, O noble people, contemplate
>   the mantra *So'ham*.
> Become aware of the mantra *So'ham*.
> The fingers do not have to move on the mala.
> The tongue does not have to make a sound.
> The unrepeated mantra is going on within you
>   all the time.
> Watch it.
> With the sound *so*, breathe out.
> With the sound *ham*, breathe in.
> Day and night, whether you are awake or asleep,
>   the mantra constantly goes on within you.
> Twenty-one thousand six hundred times a day,
>   this mantra goes on.
> Contemplate it with joy, all the time.

Brahmananda said, "As you contemplate this mantra, you attain the supreme state." Namdev, another great saint, said, "Just keep repeating *So'ham, So'ham* all the time, and you yourself will become God." This mantra has the power to transform you completely.

SIDDHA YOGA

AS YOU KEEP REPEATING THE MANTRA, through the Guru's grace you become aware that it is going on within. Then the inner Kundalini energy, which has been dormant, awakens automatically.

The Upanishads say:

bibharti kundalī shaktir ātmānam hamsamāshritā hamsah prānāshrayo nityam prānāh nādipathāshrayāh hamsavidyāmavijñāya muktau yatnam karoti yah sa nabhobhakshanenaiva kshunnivrittim karishyati

The Kundalini Shakti operates through the power of *Hamsa,* which is not different from the Self. *Hamsa* flows with the prana, and the prana flows through the nadis. One who strives for liberation without knowing the science of *Hamsa* is like one who tries to satisfy his hunger by eating the sky.

When, through the practice of *Hamsa*, the inhalation and exhalation become balanced, and the breath is retained in spontaneous kumbhaka, the breath, which has been going in and out through the *idā* and *pingalā* nadis, moves into the *sushumnā*, the central channel. The inner Kundalini, which has been dormant, becomes active and begins to unfold. Then a self-born yoga, the yoga of the Siddhas, takes place within you.

The awakening of Kundalini brings about the completion of the spiritual journey. Until Kundalini awakens, you practice yoga by your own efforts and according to your own whim. But after Kundalini has awakened naturally, yoga takes place according to the inspiration of God. It goes on in a spontaneous manner, while you go about your daily life. Kundalini is the energy which has created the entire universe, and when it is awakened within you, it works with its full power. From its seat at the base of the spine in the spiritual center known as *mūlādhāra*, it rises and begins to travel higher and higher, until it has reached the highest spiritual center, the *sahasrāra*, in the crown of the head. Moving within the body, it causes yoga postures and pranayama to take place spontaneously, as they are necessary. It purifies the blood and the bodily fluids and makes the body strong and free of disease. It stills the mind and focuses the attention within. Meditation occurs naturally, and knowledge arises on its own.

As Kundalini unfolds, the inner world is revealed to you. Every day you have new realizations which fill you with wonder. On the outside, you can watch pictures on television, but when Kundalini works within, you see pictures inside, on the inner screen. Outside, you use the telephone. But on the inside, through the inspiration of Kundalini, you attain clairaudience. I am not telling you an amusing story. I am telling you what exists inside you. When you lose your inner worth, you become the slave of external things and lose the awareness of the inner world. But through the inner Shakti you come to know what truly exists within you.

The world of yoga is full of amazing things. As Kundalini unfolds, you see new colors and scintillating inner lights. You hear exquisite divine sounds — nowhere in the outer world can you hear such music as arises in the inner realm. You taste subtle nectars, flavors more delicious than anything that can be found in this world. You smell celestial fragrances. As you turn inside, through the wonder of Kundalini, you can see the entire universe inside yourself. Sitting quietly by yourself, you travel to different inner worlds. On the outside all these worlds are far away from you, but on the inside they are very near.

Once someone showed me a Japanese radio. It was only two and a half inches long. When I moved the dial from Japan to America, the distance between Japan and America was a fraction of an inch. The distance was so small! It took me almost twenty hours to fly from Japan to America, but with that gadget it took me so little time. I moved the needle just a fraction of an inch, and America was right there. Similarly, the deeper you go inside in meditation, the closer these worlds will appear to you. You

will hear everything on the inside from very close. You will
see everything from very close. This is the mystery and
the greatness of Siddha Yoga. If the inner world did not
contain all this, why should we spend so much time in
meditation?

Inside, there is so much bliss. You constantly try to
find happiness in the pleasures of the world, but truly the
bliss you are looking for is inside. As Kundalini unfolds,
that bliss reveals itself more and more. Love for all creatures begins to pulse within, and happiness bubbles up
continuously.

Finally, as you pursue this self-born yoga, as the inner
Shakti unfolds, you reach the sahasrara, the topmost
spiritual center in the crown of the head. This is the culmination of your spiritual journey, and here the light of the
Self reveals itself. In the sahasrara there is a divine effulgence. That light has the radiance of a thousand suns. In
that center, there is no pain and no pleasure. Only the bliss
of Consciousness exists there. In the center of that divine
effulgence in the sahasrara, there is a tiny subtle blue light,
which yogis call the *nīla bindu*, the Blue Pearl. Watching
this tender, infinitely fascinating light, you become aware
of your true glory. Though smaller than a sesame seed, the
Blue Pearl contains the entire universe. It is the light of
God, the form of God within you. This is the divinity, this
is the greatness, that lies within a human being. This is the
true wonder of humanity. Therefore, perceive that light.
Just by looking at your face in the mirror, you will never
know yourself. Only if you discover that light will you

recognize who you really are. It was after seeing that light that the great ecstatic being Mansur Mastana said, "*ana'l-Haqq*," I am God. After seeing that, the great Shankaracharya said, "I am Brahman, I am the Absolute." With the awareness of that, Jesus said, "The kingdom of God is within." God's kingdom does not lie only within Jesus or within these other great beings. It is inside you and inside me and inside everyone.

One day, in meditation, the tiny blue light, the light of the Self, expands to fill the universe, and then you experience your all-pervasiveness. You attain the state of the supreme Truth, the state beyond all pain and pleasure. You experience the true bliss of Consciousness. You know without any doubt, "I am God, and God is me." From then on, you live in constant awareness of the Self, in the state of perfect fearlessness and freedom.

This is liberation. This is what you attain through the practice and the understanding of *Hamsa*. This is the secret of a Siddha's sadhana. This is the practice of perfected beings. This is the wisdom of the greatest saints. Practice it with great reverence. There is no greater mantra than *Hamsa*, no greater worship than meditation, no greater deity than the Self. Always remember this. It is the final instruction of the Guru, the command of Shiva.

The science of *Hamsa* is the science of the Self. It is the source of all knowledge. It is God's gift to us. Repeat *Hamsa* with respect.

Sit very quietly. Become aware of the breath coming in and going out, repeating *Hamsa, Hamsa.* Understand that *ham* is the perfect "I," the pure Consciousness. Understand that *sa* is the universal energy. Focus subtly on the place where these syllables arise and subside, and you will know the Self. This is the true state of God. You are That.

NOTES

1. *Shiva Sūtras* 3:43.
2. *Bhagavad Gītā* 10:25.
3. Abhinavagupta, quoted in Maheshwarananda, *Mahārthamañjari*.
4. *Bhagavad Gītā* 6:21.
5. *Shiva Sūtras* 2:1.
6. *Shri Tantra Sadbhava*.
7. *Vijñāna Bhairava* v. 24.
8. Kallata, *Tattvārtha Chintāmani*.
9. *Shiva Sūtras* 1:4.
10. *Shri Kanti-Samhitā*.
11. Patanjali, *Yoga Sūtras* 1:2

Glossary

AGAMAS
Sacred texts of the Shaiva tradition of India, considered to be divinely revealed.

ASHTAVAKRA
Literally, "deformed in eight places." A great sage of ancient times; author of the *Ashtavakra Gītā*, an important work which explains the path to God-realization.

AYURVEDIC MEDICINE
The ancient Indian science of health, still practiced, which is based on Vedic scriptures.

BHAGAVAD GITA
One of the world's greatest works of spiritual literature, in which Lord Krishna explains the path of liberation to Arjuna. The *Bhagavad Gītā* is part of the Sanskrit epic the *Mahābhārata*.

BHAGAWAN NITYANANDA
(d. 1961) Swami Muktananda's Guru and predecessor in the Siddha lineage. Also known as Bade Baba, he was a born Siddha, living his entire life in the highest state of Consciousness. His *samādhi* shrine is in the village of Ganeshpuri, a mile from Gurumayi's Ashram.

BRAHMANANDA
(19th century) Poet-saint of Rajasthan, India.

DHARANA
A centering or meditation exercise designed to give the immediate experience of union with God.

DVADASHANTA
Refers to different places inside and outside the body which, according to the Shaiva yogic tradition, are significant in the practice of yoga.

EKNATH MAHARAJ
(1528-1609) A poet-saint of Maharashtra, India.

GANESHPURI
A village north of Bombay in Maharashtra, India, near Gurudev Siddha Peeth, the main ashram of Siddha Yoga.

GARBHA UPANISHAD
An Upanishad, which gives an elaborate description of the physical body and how the soul abides in it and longs for liberation. *See also* Upanishads.

GURU
A Self-realized Master having the capacity to awaken the dormant spiritual energy of a disciple and guide him or her to the state of the Truth.

GURU GITA
An ancient Sanskrit hymn that describes the nature of the Guru and the Guru-disciple relationship. It is chanted every morning in Siddha Yoga ashrams.

IDA
A subtle energy channel of the body which originates at the base of the spine and terminates at the left nostril.

JANAKA
A saint and king of Mithila in ancient India. His Guru was Yajnavalkya; his daughter Sita, Lord Rama's consort.

JNANESHWAR MAHARAJ
(1275-1296) A great saint of Maharashtra in India whose commentary on the *Bhagavad Gītā*, the *Jñāneshwarī*, is considered one of the most important scriptural works of India.

KABIR
(1440-1518) A great mystic and poet who lived in Benares and was a weaver by trade.

KALIDAS
(ca. fifth century) A great classical poet of India; author of many plays and poems.

KARMA
Action; or effect of one's accumulated past actions.

KASHMIR SHAIVISM
A nondual philosophy which is the basis of many Siddha Yoga teachings. It recognizes the universe as a manifestation of the one divine conscious energy.

KRISHNA
The eighth major incarnation of Lord Vishnu, whose life is described in the *Mahābhārata* and whose teachings are contained in the *Bhagavad Gītā*.

KUNDALINI
The spiritual energy which lies coiled at the base of the spine of every individual. When awakened, it rises through the *sushumnā nādī*, purifying the

system through a series of spontaneous spiritual processes that lead eventually to the state of God-realization. See also *sushumnā nādī*.

MALA
A string of beads, similar to a rosary, used when performing mantra repetition.

MANSUR MASTANA
Sufi mystic of the ninth century.

NAMDEV
(1270-1350) A poet-saint of Maharashtra; a tailor by trade and contemporary of Jnaneshwar.

OM
The primal sound from which the entire universe emanates. It is the essence of all mantras.

PATANJALI
A great fourth-century sage and the author of the *Yoga Sūtras*.

PINGALA
A subtle energy channel of the body which originates at the base of the spine and terminates at the right nostril.

PRANAYAMA
A yogic technique consisting of systematic regulation and restraint of the breath, which leads to purification of the body and steadiness of mind.

PRASAD
A blessed or divine gift; often refers to food that has first been offered to God.

SADHANA
The practice of spiritual discipline.

SADHU
A holy being or monk.

SAMADHI
A state of meditative union with the Absolute.

SANNYASA
Monkhood.

SANNYASI
One who takes vows of renunciation in the Indian tradition.

SHAIVISM
See Kashmir Shaivism.

SHAKTI
Spiritual power; the divine energy that creates, maintains, and dissolves everything in the universe; or the spouse of Shiva.

SHAKTIPAT
Literally, the "descent of grace." The transmission of spiritual power or Shakti from Guru to disciple, awakening the disciple's dormant spiritual energy, Kundalini. *See also* Kundalini; Shakti.

SHANKARACHARYA
(788-820) Founder of the Advaita (nondual) school of

Vedanta, and one of the acknowledged great philosophers of India.

SHIVA

The supreme Principle of the universe, who is transcendent and immanent; the supreme Self.

SHIVA SUTRAS

A ninth-century Sanskrit text revealed to the sage Vasuguptacharya. It is the scriptural authority for the philosophic school of Kashmir Shaivism.

SIDDHA

A perfected being; one who has attained the state of unity-consciousness or enlightenment.

SIDDHA YOGA

A path to union of the individual and the Divine, which begins with Shaktipat, the inner awakening by the grace of a Siddha Guru. Swami Muktananda's successor, Swami Chidvilasananda, is the living Master of this path.

SPANDA KARIKAS

A ninth-century scripture written by Vasuguptacharya which describes how a yogi who remains alert can perceive the divine Principle in daily life.

SUNDARDAS

(1596-1689) North Indian poet-saint.

SUSHUMNA

The central and most important of the channels of the subtle body, extending from the base of the spine to the top of the head. It is through the sushumna that the awakened Kundalini energy rises.

TANTRA

A scriptural text revealed by Lord Shiva in the form of a dialogue with his consort Parvati.

UPANISHADS

Ancient scriptures in the form of dialogues between sages and their disciples, which describe the nature of the Absolute and the means for attaining it.

VEDAS

Ancient Indian scriptures, regarded as divinely revealed.

YOGA SUTRAS

A collection of aphorisms on yoga written by the great fourth-century sage Pantanjali.

YOGI

One who practices yoga.

FURTHER READING

SWAMI MUKTANANDA

Ashram Dharma
Play of Consciousness
From the Finite to the Infinite
Where Are You Going?
I Have Become Alive
The Perfect Relationship
Reflections of the Self
Secret of the Siddhas
Selected Essays
Kundalini
Mystery of the Mind
Does Death Really Exist?
Light on the Path
Lalleshwari
Mukteshwari
Meditate
What Is an Intensive?

SWAMI CHIDVILASANANDA

Inner Treasures
My Lord Loves a Pure Heart
Kindle My Heart
Ashes at My Guru's Feet
Resonate with Stillness
(with Swami Muktananda)

You may learn more about the teachings and
practices of Siddha Yoga Meditation by contacting:

SYDA Foundation
371 Brickman Rd.
P.O. Box 600
South Fallsburg, NY 12779-0600, USA

Tel: (914) 434-2000

or

Gurudev Siddha Peeth
P.O. Ganeshpuri
PIN 401 206
District Thana
Maharashtra, India

For further information about books in print
by Swami Muktananda and Swami Chidvilasananda,
and editions in translation, please contact:

Siddha Yoga Meditation Bookstore
371 Brickman Rd.
South Fallsburg, NY 12779-0600, USA

Tel: (914) 434-0124